OTHER BOOKS BY ASA

First Printing: 2020

ISBN 978-1-71673-774-9

Forward all inquiries to the following:

asaraywrites@gmail.com

Asa Ray Henson

P.O. Box 81

Royston, Ga 30662

Dedication

To the girls that love girls, boys that love boys, those that love both, asexuals, pansexuals, trans - anyone that's ever been oppressed for loving who you love, I hope this book finds you and reminds you that you are valid.

I am sorry for the unfairness. The way the world has tarnished the beauty of the heart. I hope one day we can all love freely and safely. I can't wait to meet you that day.

Please always remember that the heart's passion starts with being kind to oneself. Do not diminish your worth, for a loving heart is ten stronger than an angry heart. Be kind to yourself and love with all that you are. The truest love you will ever find will be your own, so discover it and share it with the world.

All the best, between these pages of my heart,

Asa

REALIZATION

AND

ACCEPTANCE

DO YOU REMEMBER THE FEELING OF BEING LOST

AS IF YOU DIDN' T BELONG IN ANY CROWD

ANY GROUP

NEXT TO ANYBODY

YOU TRIED SO HARD TO GIVE YOUR HEART AWAY

ONLY FOR PEOPLE TO LOOK THE OTHER WAS AS
IF IT WERE INVISIBLE

I HOPE YOU ALWAYS GIVE YOUR HEART AWAY
WILLINGLY

WHEN THE WORLD IS COLD I HOPE YOU TAKE
YOUR SOFTNESS AND LEAVE IT ON THE
COUNTERTOP TO WARM ANYONE PASSING BY

YOU' RE NOT A MATCH LIGHTING A CANDLE

YOU' RE A GENTLE HAND REMINDING OTHERS
THAT IT IS SAFE

YOU ARE SAFE

TO BE WHO YOU WANT

TO LOVE WHO YOU LOVE

TO EXIST WITHOUT WORRY

I HOPE YOU CONTINUE TO BE THAT FOR
EVERYONE IN PASSING

IT'S YOUR WHOLE PURPOSE

LOVE ENTITY SURROUNDED

Growing up I could never quite see myself

I visibly saw what I looked like in the
mirror

But something always seemed off

Missing

I would look for myself in clothes

I would search for myself within books

Yet, I could never quite get my hands on
who I was

Looking back, I have a fond recollection
of who I was trying to be

Always peering at other women and feeling
in awe of their beauty

Like little paper crushes, I couldn't
write my words fast enough to comprehend
who I was

In a sense it was utter chaos

It took almost 20 years before I first
caught the hand of my own skin

Pulling her back into my arms as if
she'd been missing home

With my own hands wrapped around my neck
I begged her to stay

To be honest with herself when she looked
in the mirror

It's strange to see us side by side now

Peeking at the eyes that were lost for so
long

Giggling over the fact that deep down I
always knew to myself to some degree

Accepting that it was okay

Realizing that I was simply a girl who
loved girls

As a kid without a safe space to express
themselves,

To be themselves

It's hard to come to terms with being
different

I grew up in a small town where nothing
exciting ever happens

It's this little slice of southern charm
and back of the woods country where
everyone falls in step together

Church runs twice on Sunday, once on
Wednesday

You don't miss it for the world

This small town is built on being moral
and having high standards but never going
anywhere

Men love women and women love men

Simple as that

Growing up without the foundation to
safely come out

To freely love who I wish

has always made the idea of relationships
seem foreign

when I first went on a date with a girl I
remember coming home and taking the
longest shower of my life

as if I needed to physically wash the sin
off of my skin

the reality is that with each scrub I was
washing away the façade I'd painted
myself in

cleansing myself of the lies and deceit
I'd forced myself to swallow

the realization that there was nothing
wrong with loving a girl was harder than
any pill I've ever taken

it hung in my throat for almost two
decades

this false idea that I could ever belong
to this town or fit in with their moral

alignment has and will always be a prank
I've been playing on myself

on those that say hello to me in passing
when I walk down the street

being gay, a lesbian, whatever you choose
to label me - it's not as taboo as this
small town makes it seem.

I'm simply a girl from the country
waiting in excitement for the day I come
home to a beautiful wife.

Aphrodite was known as the goddess of
love

So how could I not fall in love with her

The funny thing about sexuality is that everyone has an opinion

A label

They all have this idea that if they can put you in a box then you're safe

Your sexual desires couldn't possibly seep out onto their clothing like ink from a pen

So long you're in that box

They can control you

Locked in a cage like an animal

If you're open about it, maybe just maybe it'll open up questions about their own secret desires

We couldn't have that could we?

Sexuality is nothing more than the label we give ourselves so that we can love who we wish to with hopeful thinking

Yet it's never quite safe

There will always be somebody telling you that they know more about you and how you feel than you do

It's pure bullshit

I just want to love people without the demand of everyone's eyes on me

I just want to kiss a girl and feel my heart flutter without being told I'm wrong for it

Why is that so fucking difficult for people to accept

Shouldn't we be happy that I'm sharing my heart rather than putting a knife in somebody else's?

Girls can and do love girls

Boys can and do love boys

Anyone can love anyone

Please just stop acting like you created the term love and everything associated with it has to pass the bar exam for your approval

Just let people love

Accept love

Give love

Love is love.

I don' t think as a child I ever fully
processed how dangerous it is to fall in
love with somebody of the same sex

Looking back

It almost seems like a faraway dream

As a kid I didn' t process that my crush
on the girl on the playground was
something people have lost their lives
over

It' s not something that' s taught

Fortunate, I am

I didn' t grow up feeling feverish over
the thoughts of how soft a pretty girl' s
lips looked, but I did look and wonder

Nobody told me that wars have started
over less

My luxury and opportunity to be naïve was
given to me before I was born

Provided like a good excuse on the folded
page of my latest book

While I never voiced my urges about girls, they seemed like glossed over dreams

Nothing to worry about

I didn' t have to fear for my ability to love freely until I became old enough to understand

Our world has not always been kind to those who choose to pursue their heart' s desires

Western philosophy has dictated the way we allow ourselves to love

Slashing the hopes of many in the process

Limiting our free will

In some places people still die for doing something that only impacts those involved

People are beaten and left bloody on the streets for choosing to let their heart swim in love

But I never knew that as a child

History lessons in class don' t teach you
how loving somebody warrants the value of
your life

It' s pitiful, an absolute abomination,

and I am fortunate in my setting,

but I will always choose to kiss pretty
girls and give my heart away to them

even if one day it ends me. I will fight
for those without that luxury, because
they too deserve to love in peace.

It's strange how we are taught to break
our own hearts

How we're given this molding in life
that we must fit in

Like any book of guidelines

It needs work

As children we welcome love in like an
adult's first cup of coffee in the
morning

We give our heart to everyone in passing

Excitedly at that

As teenagers we're given rules on who
we're allowed to love

And we listen, mostly

Chipping away at the shelling that's
meant to protect it

Ignoring the pain and keeping silent when
thoughts that don't color inside of the
lines pop up

We bite our tongue and grit our teeth,
adjusting our route in life to fit those
in the guidebook

For years we abide by these invisible
laws

Letting those before us dictate who we
love

We break our own heart before we ever
truly give it away

And I think that says a lot for anyone
questioning if they're gay

We're willing to shatter that beating
ball of atoms within us to make others
happy

All because we were told we could only
love those chosen for us

My heart is tired and tattered from
loving people that never meant it well

From being handled by those I didn' t
truly love

Loving who I wish to feels like waking up
from a bad dream

I' ve ripped up the map I was given in
adolescence, tossing it out for the wind
to take

And because of that

My heart is slowly healing

Slowly beating again in love for the girl
I' ll one day give it to.

Eden would have smiled at my ability to
love and smile through lackluster moments

My ability to fuck without fearing the
first cast stone

Eden would've laughed at the way
everyone called me sinister for acting on
my desires

Hell, the townspeople would burn me at
the stakes if they could get away with it

But I refuse to live a life that chooses
to worship everything but your own
happiness

A life that will not accept you if
you're not their version of purity

It's as if I've woken from a dreamstate
to find that I am in full control of my
body and the soft touches that make it
shake in delight

Who would've ever thought that a woman
would be my favorite taste

That she would make me shake and almost
lose the hand I've been dealt

She would make me be willing to give up control

If only to love her in spite of what the world dictates as 'right'

Run as fast as you can for the hills
where your dreams reside

Chase them with every ounce of your being

Even if it's just a dream where you can
hold her hand and walk down the sidewalk
in peace.

They tried to mold me into their perfect
vision of a woman

With dresses hanging off of shoulders

Words crisp and soft

My voice saccharine just the way they
liked

They tried to make me into somebody
perfect for them

As if they could assemble me like a body
they built for their own pleasures

But I spoke too loud

I showed too much skin

My words weren' t sweet, they were heavy
with anger

With want and talks of more than their
golden dreams

I cursed

I bit

I spit

At all of the things they tried to make
me

And when I kissed a girl in front of
them, in the public eye

They pretended they' d never known me

That I showed an error message

Another mistake

Another body down the drain

So they tried to box me back up and send
the package back to the factory

Marking me as a discontinued item to
remove from the shelves

All for being myself.

She called to me in a dream

Asking if I had ever been in love

Her words were like thorns in my side

Prodding me like a wild animal

Encouraging me to tell her where my heart currently resided

In daylight it could almost be seen as a simple question

Another light comment asking what everyone wanted to know

In darkness it was a steel rod stabbing me in warning

I would love who I was told

I would allow them to do what they wished to me

I would let the girl holding my heart go

Pretending like her laughter never made my chest pitter patter in excitement

I woke up afraid

Terrified to be open

Scared to be honest

So I hid her

I pretended that I had never met her

Looking the other way when we walked by
each other on the street

And she grew tired of waiting

Handing me my heart back in a perfectly
wrapped box

"I' m sorry, but I can' t do this
anymore. I don' t deserve to live behind
closed doors. Neither do you. I just hope
you realize that one day" .

I do.

I realize it now

I' m sorry I couldn' t love you in the
open

the way you deserved

I' m sorry I held your heart away from me
like it oozed blood, when you held mine
against your chest warmly.

I have never felt more disgusted with
myself than the day
I kissed my girlfriend and her mother
looked at us with such illness and
told her I could either go or she could
find a new place to live

The first time I ever kissed a girl it
felt like my heart had flown through my
ribcage

and was sprinting down the highway in its
latest attempt to escape me

She tasted of nothing special, salt maybe

But my god it felt more addicting than
any bottle of alcohol I've ever put
between my lips

Her laughter warmed my soul faster than
any beer that's ever slid down my throat

If I could've spent the rest of my days
living on the clouds of her I would've
given up every dream to pursue her

I knew, without a doubt, she was only the
beginning of the awakening that'd been
happening inside of me for far too long

They taught me to cling to what was safe

So when I clung to her hips with her
tongue between my teeth

I couldn' t help but whisper how I felt
more at home in her arms than I' d ever
felt within my own skin

I think words were created to try
explaining how beautiful women are

They are the essence of the unknown
Yet they're everything I crave and love

People act as if love is like Romeo and
Juliet

A girl cannot love another girl

It's worthy of death

But maybe I would drink the poison just
to be happy and in love for a little bit

My first kiss with a girl felt like
living in a different universe

I'd fallen into a black hole of soft
whispers and gentle smiles

Existing separate from all of the things
I'd grown up being told

I suppose I expected it to feel sinful

I assumed I'd feel guilty

I felt alive

At home

Sometimes I wonder if people look at me differently

If they would deprive me of parts of the luxury I live in if they knew

They spit words of praise and gospel only to lace them with anger and hatred in the same breath

It breaks my heart to think that they will cling to a higher power

yet refuse to serve him and show kindness all because I'm a girl that wants to marry a girl

it makes me sad

I simply want to hold her hand and bring her around the people that've watched me grow

But I'll never be able to do that without there being some form of unsafety

Her hands littered my body like lights in the sky

Sparkling across my skin at nightfall

In some ways it felt like watching a firework show scatter on the 4th of July

A warmth so pleasing I would hand her the matches each time it grew dark

I look for the days where kisses are given between meals and moments of rushing out the door

Only to come home and curl up on the couch together to read

Cozying between the sheets in bed at night

Waiting for the day to repeat

Filled with love

With sincerity

Always growing

Always loving

Some people feel like sunshine

I hope we learn to love them without
force

The first girl I fell in love with amazed
me

She was full of confidence

Never doubting herself or leaving room
for people to question her

She was simply herself

Full of life

Full of laughter

I loved her for her ease

The way she made everything in life seem
so simple

As if every piece of me belonged to the
puzzle of her

She taught me a lot

Mainly she taught me to love hard and
never swallow parts of myself to please
anyone else

Misunderstood is a concept I know too
well

Branding myself with labels for the sole
purpose of making myself known to society

If you look close enough my skin is
dotted with ink and lines scratching out
the details of my growth and changes as I
age

Always adhering to the standards set by
the world

Always imprinting words on myself that
mean nothing more than a simple
definition

Begging for somebody to simply let me
love without having to shout to the world
who and why

This constant sense of battle is
exhausting

I am just a simple girl trying to figure
my life out

Accepting love as it comes and goes

Always laughing at the passion that
overflows from my lips

Today I am writing my own story

Let the world tell me how I should live
and love

How I should fuck

Let them litter my words with false rules

Let them mark out who I am and tell me
how to be

I will turn the other way and start
afresh

A new page

A new story

I will write to my heart's content

And love the girl that I wish to love

My biggest fear is winding up in a
relationship I'm unhappy with

Being tethered to a soul that my heart
doesn't ache for

Sleeping with somebody that doesn't make
my legs quake and my eyes droop

Lying to my parents and saying that I'm
in love when really my heart was never
theirs

I fear I will settle for something that
doesn't warm my soul

I'd rather never fall in love again or
fall in love and have my heart broken
than pretend I belong with somebody
unworthy of my time

Look perfect

Curl your hair

Sit up straight

Wear makeup, but not too much

Present yourself the way a respectful
woman would

Bite your tongue

Lower your voice

Stick to these rules and when somebody
calls you a name so despicable it burns
beneath your skin like lit coal for days

Smiles and acknowledge that you've done
something wrong even though you haven't

You will act accordingly and do as
you're told

Even when everything inside of you is
screaming against your bones so loud that
it tastes like bile in your throat

After all, you were made to obey

Born to recreate

Just do what you're supposed to···

Fuck you to everyone that spends their
time molding young girls into what you
think they should become

We are strong

We are full of pride and more than a
convenience when we're following orders

We are diligent and smart, brave and soft

Fuck you for ever trying to silence our
voices when we deserve to be heard

Fuck you fuck you fuck you

I will be who I wish to be.

She kissed me and my heart sped up

It raced along the roads of my ribs,

Pedal pushed flat against the beating
floorboard

Honking and flashing its lights to say

I' m in love

Kiss me again

She kissed me and my heart pounded so
hard I thought I would pass out from the
ache of it hitting the inside of my chest
so hard

Hit

Hit

Hit

Tell her you love her

She kissed me and I felt like every
moment in my life had happened solely to
bring me here

To kiss her

To laugh on her lips and to pull her back
in the second she started pulling away

Suffocate me with your kiss

I told her

I love you

I loved her

I fell in love with her as I began
falling in love with myself

Healing the nicks between my bones

I began to feel whole again

You see, I was never taught to love
myself before another person

But I am less afraid of love now that I
know my own worth

Now that I am determined to marry the
girl of my dreams

I have never felt as lost in life as I
did trying to teach myself that it was
okay to be gay

Being young and uncertain in following
what your own heart is telling you can be
the loneliest feeling

I wish somebody would' ve looked at me
and whispered it would all be okay

That one day I would wake up full of
bravery and courage

Comfortable in who I am

Loving myself in my own skin

I won't say she tasted like honey the way other stories do

But I will admit that she tasted like happiness

Between her legs I found the map to my own heart

I fell in love

I fell in love

Oh my god

She filled my days with light

Showering me in kindness and soft touches

Kissing away the thoughts when they were
so harsh I could barely breathe

She filled my days with laughter

Rolling her eyes at bad jokes and
reminding me she loved me regardless

Finding something good between the
unknown moments of each day

Silencing the chaos when needed

She taught me many things about myself

Never questioning my decisions or asking
for anything in return

When we broke up, she kissed me once and
said she would always love me

And because of her, I love myself the way
I should've always loved her

She kept her promises and continues to
help me keep mine

Be yourself. Love hard. Walk away from
the people that limit you.

It's as if you're expected to lick your wounds from the words people spit at you

Cover yourself with the person you're going to connect with

Don't let them see too much, they might run away scared

Why is it that we love behind walls of shelter, waving through the windows in blurred images

Don't you wish to kiss fiercely and to shout your lovers name so that everyone knows you're in love?

Her tongue felt like a dagger gliding
across my neck while her mouth whispered
unholy things between my ears

I still hear her words late at night when
I'm between my bedsheets and the world
is quiet

Beckoning to me

Calling for me to come out

Is this what it means to love a Siren

I'll admit that curiosity has gotten the best of me once or twice

Fooling me into believing tales of mischief and horror

Misguiding me towards mistakes that will follow my name forever

But it's never done wrong by my heart

Curiosity may have killed the cat, but it was the very key that unlocked my beating atoms from their cage and said

Go forth my child

Love her with all that you are

It's okay

In high school, in the office waiting for the guidance counselor,

a girl asked me if I liked girls and I panicked

denying it with every ounce of my being

Terrified that she could see right through my lies

She told me it was okay if I did,

I denied it once more

Then it happened again

and again,

people asking

Each time filling me with anxiety and each time forcing me to make

up lies,

so afraid that anyone who found out would tell the school

and I would be shunned

My friends would joke and question me
whenever I said a girl

looked pretty, and it would petrify me to
think I' d almost gotten

caught

I' d go home and lay in bed at night
wishing I could say yes,

Just once

Looking back, we were just kids that knew
nothing about love

Most of the kids I went to school with
probably would' ve supported me

It didn' t impact them to the point that
they' d care, but it felt

like the biggest secret

It felt so heavy walking the halls day
after day,

lying

I tried so hard to tell the people I was close with, only for them

to remind me it was a sin

To shut me back into my dark corner, my web of lies

I wish the young me, who was so insecure and filled with anxiety,

I wish she felt strong

Like she could love anyone deserving of her heart

I wish she didn' t have to lie

5th Grade:

I thought they were beautiful and wanted to tell them, but I bit my tongue

6th Grade:

She looked so cute when she was embarrassed, and I wanted to slip her a note saying so. I buried the note in my backpack

7th Grade:

Somebody asked me who I thought the prettiest in our grade was. I wanted to tell them her name, but lied and said I'd never thought about it, there were a lot of pretty girls in our class.

8th Grade:

We talked about cute boys in bands and shared posters of male idols from magazines. I kept the ones of girls for myself at home.

9th Grade:

I walked the halls with the same students, meeting people older than me. A boy I grew up with was asked if he was gay, so he waited until we were in drama class and made out with a girl behind the curtains. We both knew he was hiding himself.

10th Grade:

I dated a girl from another city with a boy's name so that when people asked I could tell them I had plans with my boyfriend. I never told her. We broke up.

11th Grade:

I no longer had to walk the hallways with curious eyes. My work was done from home. When my friends came for a visit, we talked about my health to avoid talking about love.

12th Grade:

I graduated a little sooner than my classmates and went to the beach rather than walking with them. Disconnecting felt easier than seeing them again and lying.

Age 18-21:

I say hey to my friends from school in passing when I see them in town. They show off their wedding rings and introduce me to their kids. I tell them I'm too busy working to date.

Age 22-23:

I introduce a girl to my mom for the first time. I share pictures of us on social media and my high school friends all tell me they're happy for me. She breaks my heart 8 months later. But that's okay because I'm no longer lying. I'm not hiding anymore. I'm not afraid to date a girl and to be proud of her. It feels right.

Fear seems trivial when you realize
children are tamed to fit a specific
molding,

Taught that heterosexuality is normal and
anything outside of that is different,

It' s not surprise that sexual
orientation is seen as such a hostile
situation,

Making anyone that doesn' t fit the
outline feel like an outcast from the
moment they start to speak

It' s saddening to watch so much love
wash away as if it were sand on your
driveway,

Removed and prohibited solely because
somebody once said anything outside of
their heteronormative beliefs was
shameful,

And everyone around them nodded their
heads to agree rather than taking the
time to understand or speak up and
correct them

My sexuality

The sexuality of others

It is not something that can be bought
like a toy in a kid's store

You don't try to remove it from somebody
like a fake tattoo on skin

It is part of me, whether you wish to
accept it or not

Stop analyzing how others love and be
happy they're willing to love rather
than seek revenge and fight

Magnificent is what I would' ve told them
of our love

It was like summer rain washing down over
you after you ran your hardest towards
shelter to beat the storm

Never truly calm

Always pounding inside of me

Swirling like a riptide taking you out to
sea

I would look at you and the chaos in my
mind would cease momentarily

So if they asked me, what I thought of
our love

I would tell them it was magnificent

Everything we both needed at that time

And even when they looked the other way
when we kissed, I would kiss you again
ten seconds longer

We deserved to love hard too

If love is painful why do we chase it

If it banishes us from circle cliques and
prevents us from having our dream job
then why do we still ache for it

Why do I ache for the touch of her gentle
hands around my neck moments after her
lips were there sharing secrets

If loving this way is so wrong then why
does it feel like each time she tells me
she loves me I can breathe a little
easier

Tell me

Please tell me

Why is she the forbidden fruit

We both know I'm going to take the bite

So many before me have fought

They have been reckless and in love

Shouting it to the skies

Only to be beaten down in bloodshed for wishful thinking

They have fought battles I can' t even taste

Prying their way into a temporary space of safety

Where they are free to love

They have fought them for themselves as much as they have fought them for me

I will never be able to express my gratitude to those that' ve given their lives for me to be able to kiss a girl in broad daylight should is so choose

They tried to tame my tongue the same way
the tried to tame my mouth

Washing it with soap and projector screen
guidelines

Making me rehearse right from wrong

Coercing me in attempt to make my heart
obey

But when she walked in, so full of beauty

Her presence was ethereal

It lit the dainty walls of my heart as
soon as she unlocked it

Beckoning me to let the beating vessel
inside talk

She said to listen closely to what it had
to say

And it told me the secrets they'd locked
away

  'you were made to love her, love her
right'

The first girl I had sex with never made
me feel ashamed

She kissed me so softly it felt like the
guilt melted away

When I felt scared and roamed back
towards the road I'd been told to follow

She walked along beside me, never
belittling me

We walked so long my limbs were sore

So she helped me pause to rest, holding
me more than before

Her patience taught me love greater than
I've ever known

If it weren't for her, I'd probably
still be on that road, lost looking for
an unknown door

She loved me through my sorrow and my
denial

Never getting angry at me even though I
was a child

We were both so young so full of life

I hope she fell in love with somebody
that deserved to be her wife

Thank you for the time you spent loving
me

For being kind and understanding when I
wasn't ready

Thank you for never pushing beyond my
boundaries

And for helping me find comfort in who I
longed to be

Do you dream of the day when you wake up beside the one you' ve been dancing around days waiting for?

I hope they' re kind to you.

I hope they treat you with respect and always try to communicate when life gets chaotic.

I hope that when you wake up next to them this world isn' t so cruel and filled with hatred for things that should' ve never been made out to be evil.

I hope you are free to love with all that you have with whoever you have.

Love was never meant to be locked away
like a painting at a museum

It was meant to be shown in the softest
and brightest colors we can see in

It was meant to be felt in the darkest
moments of the night

It was never meant to be limited to
whatever this is that we've created

Break the mold Break the mold Break the
mold

Family dinners have always been uncomfortable, reeling me in for questions about who my boyfriend is. My childhood was never disrupted in the sense that I brought boys home for my mother to meet. Over the holidays, I never bought cologne or looked for the perfect gift for the perfect guy. When we dined with my aunts and uncles, the questions were limited, always focused on the conservative side of things. I wanted to so badly to tell them about the pretty girl I saw walking in to eat, and politely remove myself from the room to ask her number. Instead I found myself pushing a smile up and making the excuse that I didn' t have time to date. If only I could' ve talked about how excited it made me to think about the woman I would one day marry without the fear of destroying the traditions we' d set. I would' ve loved to tell them I couldn' t wait to meet a girl to bring to our annual meet ups and show her off.

Beneath my bedsheets I've always
expressed myself better

I've devoted myself to exploring my
identity

Allowing curiosities to find their answer

Out in the daylight I always had to be
quiet

Biting my tongue and watching what I said

But beneath my bedsheets my words are
able to express their feelings freely

They're allowed to be as loud as they
wish

As blunt as they desire

Beneath my bedsheets I found freedom

It's a shame that in conservative towns the answer to sexual identity is therapy

If I remember correctly, I labeled myself as gay/queer/lesbian because of past trauma

And while I was definitely traumatized from a childhood I wouldn't wish to relive

I know without a doubt that I always wanted to kiss girls long before my body was touched without consent

My father made me hide the secrets of a brother with evil in his heart

And while therapy has helped me address my emotions towards the scars deep inside, and I no longer resent my father nor my brother

I can't deny that I've looked at girls since childhood and thought about how soft their lips look

Therapy be damned for my sexual identity
has always run rampant through my veins

Today it screams

'Girls Girls Girls'

We live in a world so focused on the way people wish to love that we often abandon those we claim we're in love with.

Didn't your mother ever teach you that imposing on somebody else's relationship is dangerous?

You teeter on the outside of the line, looking in from the window

Questioning the heart that just wants to be happy

Yet you're forgetting about the one back at home waiting on you day after day

Missing out on the time and energy you could spend on them because you're too busy trying to destroy something that doesn't belong to you

Sharing may be caring, but I promise I'll share my thoughts with you the second you intervene in my right to love

I have forgiven those that' ve been cruel
to me,

That' ve been forceful with me

You see, their ignorance doesn' t deserve
a permanent placement in my timeline

They were momentary lapses of pain and I
refuse to carry the weight of their
burden with me for the rest of my life

I refuse to pass that pain on for the
next generation to come

Should anyone ever listen to my words and
allow them to take impact, I do not want
the negativity from somebody' s stupidity
to linger in those words

I don' t want them to take the pain I
felt from somebody' s lack of compassion
to alter their ability to have hope in
loving who they wish

I only wish for them to feel free in
being themselves and showing kindness to
the next person

Those that've been cruel will not break me

I will spit and fight to regain my hopeful heart every single time

Afterall, love is everything and not everyone deserves mine

Heteronormative love never made me whole

The romantic gestures felt like ice on my
neck and as hard I tried my eyes would
always stray

You see, while I struggled to find the
words to admit to myself more than others

I always knew I would never be happy
marrying a man

If it happened then it would be a forced
love

It would be dishonest

Only done for the happiness of those
around me

Why can't we normalize chasing after
those that make our hearts flutter
regardless of their gender rather than
creating this façade that feels so
uncomfortable I'd rather go missing

I'm sorry to the boys I couldn't love,
but I'm thankful that I didn't hold you
hostage in a relationship where we were
lying to each other

It's kind of funny that my first
'boyfriend' came out of the closet
before I did

How we both turned out to be gay

Perhaps that's why we got along to begin
with

Kindred spirits hiding in the closet
together

Waiting for the chance to walk out into
the light and say, 'we should break up
and see other people. Maybe people of the
same sex'.

People in my hometown would rather scream about the fact that I love a girl than put the local pedophile on trial for doing the unforgivable

They would rather cut off my opportunities to be myself than discuss the couple having an affair

While I simply want to live a life of happiness with the girl I marry, they would rather me move off and never bring her around than reach out to help the addict begging for somebody to care

My sexuality is more important to them, it's more of a sin to them, than looking at anything else going on in this town

How fucked up is that

Sometimes I feel like Aphrodite

Standing on a pedestal for people to watch

Picking at and prodding like an animal pinned to the wall

They want me to be silent for the mistreatment of those that don't have a voice

They want me to fall in line and follow the way they've deemed I should live my life

I refuse to be controlled by an audience that that can't even comprehend how to be kind to each other

It's a damn shame I'm surrounded by people that focus on what I'm doing and who I'm fucking more than they focus on the dreams they could achieve if they spent time following their own fucking dreams.

Did you know that it takes less than 15 seconds to tell somebody you could love them

But it takes years to get over the trauma of somebody pushing your identity back down your throat each time you try to self identify

More people in the lgbtqia community wind up in abusive relationships because they spend so many years being mistreated for trying to just be who they are

Those years battling to be free not only scar them, but they push them to be blind to their own worth

Stop treating other people's identity like a piece of paper that you can tear up and toss in the trash

Encourage others to be who they want to be

To explore the things they're curious about

Rather than bottling it up and getting hurt trying to be fucking happy with the fact that they might have a chance to be out

Help build them up and remind them not to settle

Everyone deserves a chance at love

A chance to be happy and treated well

Love does not mean you won't get hurt

It doesn't mean it'll last forever

Love isn't a promise that things will be easy and you'll always have the answers

It's risky

It's scary sometimes

But it's something that we all deserve a chance at

Go ask that girl you have a crush on if you can take her for coffee

If she rejects you, at least you tried

Go kiss the boy you went on a secret date with and ran from when the time came to say goodnight

You shouldn't have to hide

Go after them, they're deserving of love as much as you are

I am so exhausted seeing people love from afar because so many in the world refuse to let us live our lives behind closed doors

Love was never meant to be hidden

It was meant to be explored and
experienced

To be filled with lessons and growth

Each day that we don't allow somebody to
experience love

We're preventing them from reaching
their full potential

We are keeping them from something that
might become their safe haven

Please stop holding people back from love

I am thankful to the girls I have dated

The ones that' ve loved me regardless of my flaws

As well as the ones that haven' t been loyal or ready to love me the way I deserve

Each of you have been impactful for me

You' ve been part of my growth

My well being

In everything we went through together

I am eternally grateful for the time we had

Things haven' t always been perfect, but they' ve been real

You are part of the reason that I feel comfortable looking for the day I marry the girl that steals my heart

You are the reason I feel like I can walk outside and up to a girl and tell her she' s pretty just because she deserves to hear it

Living so many years afraid to be open
with my heart felt like living without
the light on

If I had never found the courage to allow
myself to be free, I wonder if I would
still be walking around blindly

SELF CARE

AND

KINDNESS

I have found a home in letting myself feel

There's something comforting about allowing your emotions to flow without pushing them away or running in the opposite direction

If only I had understood how to process the things I feel when I was younger

Perhaps I would be in another country taking picture of a girl I'm in love with

All I know that I'm not even being kind to myself in allowing this

I'm simply treating myself with decency

Something we all forget to do

Take care of yourself

You are valid

Self care for me often looks like curling
up beneath the sheets early in the
morning, a cute girl in my arms

It doesn' t have to be romantic

I just like being the heater

Being close to something seemingly
angelic

It feels right

Dear Self,

Remember to drink water

Eat a decent meal

Run when you feel stressed

Write out your feelings when you need to decompress

Treat yourself the way you will treat any girl you fall in love with

You will learn to love yourself in
different ways throughout life

Different encounters will teach you how
to spread love across yourself like
you're buttering bread

Covering every inch of yourself in a net
of safety

You'll go through periods where it
doesn't feel deserving

But then you'll wake up one morning with
the remnants of self love as if it were a
cookie you ate right before bed

It won't always taste sweet, sometimes
it'll be bitter

But you must always choose yourself

Never stop choosing yourself

You are the only person that's with you
24/7

Learn to embrace your being

I don't think that accepting I'm gay
ever felt like a discovery necessarily

It mostly felt like a coming home party
within the confinement of myself

In some ways I walked through the front
door of my heart and said, 'it's good
to be here'

Simple as that

While learning to accept myself I also
learned to accept others

When they weren't so kind

When they didn't quite understand

I learned that they were missing out on a
relationship with me that could've been
exciting

I could write many chapters about the
people that've walked away when they've
found out I'm gay

But I'd rather close the storybook on
them and start a new tale

One where I love myself for all that I am

The women I have loved have taught me many things

How to be gentle

How to be patient

How to be sincere

How to be kind

Most importantly they've taught me how to love

To accept others even when our paths only cross momentarily or we go in different directions

To always move forward

They've taught me to accept myself

If you drew a map with directions to your
future, where would you go

Who would you love

Who would you want to remember

I want my map to lead me to myself and my
heart so I can give it away to her

It's true that I don't always know how to love myself

I still get insecure and I'm often uncertain

Just because I know where I want to be doesn't mean I know how to get there

I think that's okay

To not always have the answers

To not always know how to love yourself the right way

You don't always have to be kind

Sometimes you need to shout and scream and cry

Just take it one day at a time and do your best

Love will always find you

Buy the lingerie

Take the dirty pictures

Do whatever makes you feel like you are
deserving

You don' t have to show anybody you
don' t want to

Just do what makes you happy and be the
you that you wish to be

Share that with the people you choose to

Not who tells you the deserve you

In the years I spent hiding my identity from everyone including myself, I grew oblivious to understanding my own thoughts. I locked away my emotions and tied them neatly with ribbons in gift boxes that I thought would never see the light. I acknowledge how damaging it was to grow up unable to be myself because of the judgement from everyone else, but I am just as guilty for limiting myself. For refusing to nurture my own body and heart. I hope I never face a day again where I can't cling to my own hand in a love that runs so deep that I don't know my own self in the mirror. I want to spend my days loving myself the way I should've been taught as an adolescent. I want to rip the ribbons and tops off of the boxes of who I am and wear my skin proudly. I will I will I will.

I watch shows with lgbt representation
and it's half assed. I watch couples
receive hate and feel uncertain with who
they can show their relationship to, out
of fear that somebody will spout off hate
for no reason. It's a shame to me that
in a world where progress seems so close
in reach, we are still trying out damn
best to learn to smile and wave as people
walk by with their tongues bitten and
anger spewing.

When can we simply be happy?

I want to spoil myself in love so much
that I never lower my standards or hide
the love I share with somebody

I want to feel free in compassion and
kindness

Do you ever look at a girl and feel as if
your entire reason for existing is to
look at her?

You've lived all of these years, through
good and bad, just to pass this gorgeous
girl in the street and think 'wow,
isn' t she beautiful'

It' s as if the universe quits
functioning for a moment, the world no
longer spins

All that matters is the peacefulness of
appreciating her

I hope she has a good day today

Wherever she is

I've become indifferent about winding up
with somebody in my 20s.

Rather than chasing the idea of love and
wishful thinking, settling for somebody
as uncertain about their life as I am,
I'm comfortable waiting

Enjoying my time that's spent focusing
on myself

When I feel like the world is too much, I
will rely on my friends to ground me and
keep my heart content and safe

I will travel and explore the world
without worry

I will race towards my goals without rush

When somebody enters my life that's
worth loving, I will love them as I am at
that point in time

With kindness and who I am growing to be

I hope it shows

That the years I've spent catering to my
own desires doesn't mean I don't have
room to love

It just means I' m happy in my own
setting

And I will always chase the sunrise for a
new day

I hope they' ll join me in their own way

Take the morning to sleep in when you're too tired to think through your thoughts

Take the extra snack that you might want later in the day

Take the bath or the shower or the vacation you've been dying to go on

Be kind to yourself the way you would show somebody else love and affection

These are the moments where you will learn your value and how to stand guard around your heart

You will learn to be unapologetic for the things you feel and the way you love

Be good to yourself

Most days I spend my time writing and trying to decipher the thoughts in my head

Sometimes I wonder if I would be less critical of myself if I'd been kinder to myself growing up

I question if my depression is real, even though I know it's valid and I've been diagnosed

I worry that I won't live up to my expectations if I don't keep pushing

Often that idea leads me to my breaking point because I stop letting myself process the things I feel

I hope that the kids growing up today don't feel such pressure to identify and fit in

I hope they treat themselves with respect, and when they make mistakes they hold their head high knowing everyone that's come before them has also made mistakes

We are not perfect being

Far from it

We often shelter ourselves from the
things that are good for us out of fear
of getting hurt

While chasing the things that numb us,
out of fear of having to feel

I hope kids today won't have to feel
that pain all the time

That numbness

Maybe if they learn to accept themselves
and the changes they go through, then
perhaps they'll fall in love with all of
the tiny details that make them so
incredible

Please don't give up

Please be kind and teach children to be
soft with themselves

I wake up to watch the sunrise now,
excited for a new day

It's calming to me to witness the earth
come alive while everyone's still asleep

To sit there and think of the things
I've survived

How I'm still here when two years ago I
could've cared less if I lived or not

When I'm stressed I clean

When I'm upset I write or I read

I make time to watch the shows I wish to
see and learn the languages I want to
master

These little moments that appear like
nothing to the world are everything to me

They're the peace when the voices are
loud

They're the softness I give myself
because the world can be harsh

And I deserve a little peace

Dear Asa,

When you fall in love again, introduce to her to your mom right away. Let her see the intricacy of your family and how they're so warming to anyone you bring home.

When you fall in love again, write daily letters as you always do, but read them to her on the phone on the nights you're not together. Make sure she knows how you feel.

When you fall in love again, spend time focusing on your goals and send her simple messages to make sure she knows you haven't forgotten her. Your work is important but so is she. Find balance.

When you fall in love again, take her to meet your friends and encourage her to spend time with hers. Then talk about how much fun you had when you get back together at the end of the night. It's important to live outside of each other as much as it is to live together.

When you fall in love again, be prepared for change. Embrace it like the fall leaves and chase the chill away.

When you fall in love again, share your dreams, your past, and build your future together. Don' t hold back.

When you fall in love again, buy gifts but don' t buy too many. Save your money for trips together. That time traveling with each other is a gift in itself.

When you fall in love again, don' t be afraid to get hurt. Sometimes people are only here in passing. They' re still important to your story. Accept that and move on at your own pace.

When you fall in love again, be sure that you remember to love yourself too.

This is a reminder to drink your water and eat what you're craving.

Money comes and goes but you deserve to spoil yourself with the things you want in the moments.

Save when you can, but spend what you can't take with you.

See the world.

See yourself through your own eyes.

Embrace your infinite possibilities.

Do you show yourself pity when you fail?

Do you still wallow in the things that haven't worked out?

All of the years that've passed by, you would think you'd learned to give yourself the time you need to heal

To get back up and run the race again

No matter who breaks your heart

Always get back up

Look them in the eyes and acknowledge that you are okay whether they hurt you or not

You will continue moving forward

Chasing success

Being kind

It is frightening to review the past as
if it' s a film being played back

When certain memories resurface it takes
everything in me not to call it a day and
cry in my bed

Sometimes I choose to do that just
because I need the relief

When I look back at the traumas I have
lived through

The heartaches and misunderstood moments,

The lack of compassion,

It burns like a match stuck in my throat
that refuses to burn out

But through that pain

Through all of that ache

I am still standing

I' m able to recognize that I don' t have
to stay in situations that do not speak
kindness into my soul and encourage me to
prosper

I do not have to remain guarded towards people that refuse to be considerate over the fear of losing money or not being good enough

I determine my own worth

I set my own standards

And I choose who I'm willing to let live in the moments I choose to share

No matter the pain I have felt or the scars that act as re-opened wounds sometimes,

Every moment I haven't been okay has allowed me to give myself the patience I need when I need a moment to not be okay

Gentleness, kindness, understanding, and patience are all key to ensuring I am me and I can be me happily.

Days when I feel too tired to work

I have to remind myself that it is okay

I'm allowed to take breaks

I show myself grace and make time

To lay around and simply breathe

There are days when it's important just
to exist

I learned to accept my crushes on women
when I learned I was worthy of being
crushed on too

If sexuality were something we wore like tattoos on our skin, I would want the word gay printed across my forehead with

'I love' on one cheek and 'women' on the other.

Make it known so that everyone could see me fall to my knees in worship over the fact that I have and always will love women.

There's a girl that told me she saw through me

She laughed when I rolled my eyes and told her she knew nothing of me

Yet when I asked her to explain my being she told me everything I'd been hiding

She warned me of blocking myself from feeling

From prohibiting myself from being everything I am

She told me I needed to allow myself to feel and be who I am because I wouldn't reach my full potential otherwise

I knew she was right, and as much as I tried to ignore it

I crave to be my full self without pretending

Without limiting my opinions

My work ethic and my potential isn't defined by my personal life

But so many act as if it's everything

Do you ever look at the night sky and ask
how life would be different if you'd
have loved yourself more growing up

I do

I found beauty in the way I put a day
together when it's falling apart and
still manage to make it to the end

Do you ever search for the curiosity that allows different versions of yourself to take over

Because I do

I see them all, and I wonder who is going to win

But I always find that no matter who I wind up becoming, I am in love with women

And even when all of the version of myself collide

I am still a pawn in the universe of appreciation for love

You would think seeing the world would
have me falling in love with women around
the globe

But all I want is a woman that understand
my schedule while supporting my in my
dreams and simultaneously chasing hers

We can coexist while growing together

Just you and me

Looking back on my time growing up and my
time exploring other states

I can confidently say I balanced fucking
up and doing my best by others

My heart may have hurt at times and
needed moments to heal

But I was more than prepared to accept
that and move forward

I ached and pursued growth all at once

I needed that tine

Cali blessed me

I had to become comfortable with the knowledge that a good portion of people in my life would condemn me to hell

They would look at me with judgement and mistreat me

Today I take their peering eyes as mistaking me for somebody that cares

It took years for me to become comfortable with the idea of god again

For me to understand that my lack of a relationship or the strength of my relationship with god was only something I could contain

Only I could define it

When I finally stopped questioning myself for beliefs they didn' t abide by,

For fear of being shunned

I began to grow calm again

I felt peaceful

Sometimes I don't feel strong

I don't feel confident

I don't feel at ease

My identity seems almost foreign at times

Pressured to be something it isn't

To dress up as if Halloween is a year round event

But eventually I always settle back into my own skin

I somehow manage to find my way home

On days I don't know who I am

I'm aware that I will find the key to myself and the door it fits in at some point

I have to accept that for being something rather than nothing

It's kind of funny how I started falling in love with myself with each kiss I shared with a girl

In some ways it's as if kissing women has taught me how to be gentle with myself

Reminding me I'm not invincible and lingering as if a silent letter to be soft

Kissing men always made me feel out of place

They were so sloppy in comparison

Rough and aggressive

But kissing a girl was like opening a love letter to myself

And now I carry it with me everywhere I go

A permanent memory to never be less of myself

To never lower my standards

I wonder if other people fall in love
with people so easily

You see,

I fall in love with people daily

People in passing

Their bits and tales that grab the hand
of my story

I fall in love with store owners and
business women

My heart swooning over their small acts
of kindness

I fall in love with cultures and cities
I'm only in briefly

I fall in love with the way that life
buzzes around me

So electric that I can almost taste it

It never tastes like battery acid

It bewilders me how quickly and quietly I
love

In passing

In moments

Fragments of time allow me to appreciate people I interactive with regularly

The way that others keep moving on

Sometimes I just can' t help but stop and stare

I hope I always fall in love with the people that move about freely without knowing they' ve impacted me permanently

I hope I always love this easily

This frequently

To be in love with the life we live is great, but to be in love with life as it buzzes around us is enchanting

I hope to never wake up from this ride of wanderlust

It fuels me daily

It drives the bus

I am swallowing this love like I can' t get enough

I look at the life I've lived

Thinking of the ways I've been
influenced

Molded and shaped into a person of
uncertainty

It amazes me that as afraid of life as I
was growing up

I want to live so openly now

So careless

I want to smile at strangers in passing

Stop in small shops on the street and get
to know the employees, the owners

To thank them for their time and
compliment their business, buying what
makes me smile just to show support

I want to take care of my friends so that
they never understand financial burden or
have go without

I want to send them on trips and take
them with me on trips

There's this sense of carefulness I
lived with for so long

That now I don't know how to feel about
who I once was

Most people would call my naïve,

A fool for giving away what I earn

Or maybe they'd call me greedy for
wanting more in life so that I can give
it to others

Whatever it may be

I'm finally content in who I am and who
I'm becoming

I don't feel so frightened by the
thoughts of tomorrow

I simply want to live a life of comfort
and make sure those around me are able to
do the same

Maybe that's hopeful

Perhaps it is greedy

At the end of the day I just want
everyone safe

Words don' t sting the way they used to

I think in a sense I' ve grown cold to
taking what others spit out at me

I use it to light the fires that keep me
warm at night

Ignoring the small comments that
would' ve made me ache in anger and
confusion as a child

It' s funny how somebody can be so
dependent on telling you how to live

How you should eat, dress, talk

Without ever recognizing their own
insecurities

They get used to dictating others and
forget to be present in their own life

I will be who I wish to be

I will say what I wish to say

Regardless of what I' m told

I refused to live in a shadow of myself

To become a shell again

Today I feel calm

As if fall leaves could drop onto my skin
with comfort

The seasons will be changing soon and I
will be watching as time passes

A fake construction that only serves to
remind us that we are running out of it

That we should do the things we've
always wanted before it's too late

Today I'll love myself extra

There are parts of me that lie dormant

Changed but still the same

In some ways they' ve ceased to exist

In others they are still there in the
dark corners

Parts of who I am

Who I was

There are all of these little versions of
myself

Living inside this one home

Taking turns on who will get to exist
today

Saying goodnight when their time is over
and going to sleep to allow the next
version of me to wake up bright and early

Come morning

I hope I am myself while being new

I hope I am always me but always new

I am amazed at how soft we can all be

As humans we are inherently ourselves
when nobody is looking

Often peering at others through silence

Questioning their life and comparing it
to ours like two books on a bookstore's
shelves

When nobody is watching we're watching
others

Keeping track with each other in moments
of peace

I think that's beautiful

How we constantly put faces we'll never
see again with stories

Allowing ourselves a moment of inner
peace

A second to calm the storm of the day in
our minds and wish goodness upon somebody
we'll never know the name of

I hope we never lose that sense of
curious kindness

I've never felt more alone than when I

- Dated a girl that would only show
  affection in front of others
- Dated a girl who would've given me
  the world if she'd know who she
  was and what she wanted

  Now she calls me every few years to
  apologize for being dishonest with
  me

- Worked with a group of people that
  never asked if I was okay after I
  quit my job without saying goodbye

It's funny how you can be with and
around so many people, but feel as if you
could float off into the sky and they'd
never reach out to pull you back down

I feel less alone most of the time now

I stopped drinking when I realized that
my inner peace had burned to ashes and
I'd flooded the roads inside of me
trying to put out the flames

I'm still sorry to the people I walked
away from, but I had to let you go in
order to preserve my well being

We weren't meant to stay in each
other's lives forever

I hope you're well now

I'm better

I am whole.

Drinking became a method of coping when I stopped allowing myself to be who I've always been. I stopped letting my feelings flow freely and bottled up bits of myself to keep from stepping outside of everyone else's comfort zones. But nobody ever asked me if I was okay. They didn't check on me when I stopped being loud and became a quiet voice in my own head

Instead it took nearly ending the life I should be living happily to get back to myself.

Nobody should ever shut off themselves for the sake of somebody else.

In a way it's almost worse than drinking poison.

She danced in silver moonlight

Moving as if every fiber of her being had been created to soothe the night sky

With every step and each weave I caught a glimpse of her soul

Who she was underneath the makeup

The expensive clothing

Flashy smiles

She moved with such elegance I could've sworn she was a fairy and I'd been dreaming

She moved as if she were at home

One with the grass and dirt that clung to her bare feet

That memory replays over in my mind nightly

Misconstruing daily moments and reminding me that we are all hiding who we really are

Beneath the surface I am screaming to be unleashed

Dirty fingers scrub at my skin

Mistreating the bones beneath it

Dirty words clog my ears

Lying to the mind between them

I want so badly to be so much

While ceasing to exist at all

That sometimes I forget to step back and breathe

To let myself fall

Tie me up and bind me with my own words

Hold them against me as if it's all I'm worth

Because if we're being honest, I've never been good at much

But I could write a million words about falling in love and discovering who you are

I wish to spit them out of my mouth so fast that I don't take any with me to the grave

I once knew a girl who picked at herself
until she'd picked herself apart

She'd wake each morning and pick at her
nails

She'd brush her teeth and pick at her
hair

Her days were all the same

From picking at her nails

To picking at her clothes

Picking at her voice and picking at her
nose

She'd pick apart her brain

She'd pick apart her smile

She'd pick apart the things she loved
about herself every once in a while

By the time she'd turned into a teenager
she'd picked herself raw

Destroyed the soul that was hers to call

She'd picked so hard she couldn't see
herself in the mirror

At the end of the day all she was left
with were tears

You see, she learned from a young age
that picking at what people call flaws
would make them like her

So she picked apart everything about her

She picked at the things she once
would' ve cherished

Picked apart her thoughts until there was
nothing left

And then when everybody still didn' t
accept her, she asked the night sky what
was wrong with her

She questioned how she wasn' t perfect
enough

Never seeing that she' d been perfect
from the start

She' d picked and picked until she
didn' t recognize herself

Only to rebuild from the ground up
everything she felt

She set her goals

She set her marks

She became the person she'd wanted
everyone to love all her life

When she stopped picking at the things
nobody truly cared about

She found a happiness in herself that
never blew out

Gathering bits of myself

I often feel like a houseplant forgotten

In need of water

Desperate for sunlight and the presence
of nature

If only I remember to take care of myself
the way I take care of others

I could become far more than a dying
flower

Dear self,

Please nurture yourself extra today

There are still nights where I find
myself trapped in uncertainty

Wishing away the time just so I don't
feel as if my chest has a car sitting on
top of it right before it slides off the
edge of a cliff

I work hard

I try to be kind

I do my best at being gentle

Even when I'm hiding my own trauma
behind snarky remarks and sarcastic
banter

But there are nights when my thoughts are
still so loud that I can't seem to
escape myself fast enough

So I try not to escape

I lock the doors and board up the windows
inside, and I stay

Until the voices become silent

And my god they'll become so silent at
times that I wish I could just hear any

thought dripping like tap water in my brain

But it's quiet

Eerily so

Maybe it's my way of coming down from such a troublesome, rowdy round of fighting my own brain

Perhaps it's just exhaustion

But I crave these moments because they make me think

They give me the ability to breathe easy when my mind shifts and balances back out

They remind me not to ever assume anyone is okay

We're all lost in this world of figuring things out and taking mis-steps to get to the train headed towards the next chapter of our lives

So these moments call to me and remind me that I can be at peace during moments

But I must live and catch the door to
hold it open for somebody that isn't

Be bold

Be unafraid

Be uncertain

Most of all, be kind and try to
understand when you can

We're not all okay all of the time

Most of the time we're not okay at all

The thing about living with anxiety or
depression is that it's always there

Even during the good moments

It'll quietly trickle down from your
brain and spread like liquid chaos until
it burns your throat and carves letters
into your lungs

Living with it isn't ever easy

Sometimes I'll wake and days will seem
as if they're great, and I do enjoy my
days, but my god it feels as if I'm
suffocating on the entity of who I am

As if I can never be entirely me

Always holding back

Always prepared to scream

In a lot of ways I think the world has
made self discovery feel that way,

Never allowing people to fully dwell in
the comfort of their being

Of who they love

I am not dealing with my feelings well today, so I will be as light as I can walking through my own brain

I will be gentle and make time for myself to exist in the silence, because it feels so very loud and I am drowning in my own ocean of emotions

This is only temporary

Funny that life wasn't always this
overwhelming

How each day didn't always feel like a
quest to figure out what the fuck to do
with all of this time we're handed

Do you go to school

Do you apply for a new job

Should you take a weekend and go on an
adventure somewhere far away

What should you eat or buy at the grocery
store

How should you dress today

Most days I feel as if I can figure these
things out without it seeming burdensome,

But there are some moments when the most
I can do is get out of bed and write a
list of things I might accomplish that
day, or one day

Nobody tells you how adulthood feels like
a bad acid trip sometimes

They just tell you not to grow up

I wonder if people think about how we describe mental illnesses as if they're not tied to us directly,

Implanted inside of who we are

We've been taught to describe it as 'not feeling like ourselves' , and I'm as guilty as ever when it comes to that definition, but if we look at it, truthfully view it, those lapses in our being, when we're not okay, that sense of not being okay is just as much a part of who we are as any other emotion.

So I don't want to say like I don't feel like myself anymore, because I do

I feel it so fucking much that I don't know what to do with myself

And that's what can be exhausting

Being tied to yourself at all times

I know that it's okay to feel this way, and I understand I will have good moments as much as bad moments for the rest of my life, but sometimes I just have to think these moments through.

Otherwise I might truly go off the deep end one day and never come back

If that happens, and I don't wish for it to, I'm glad I'll be stuck with myself still

There's nobody else I'd prefer to be stuck with

Me, myself, and I.

I am my own team, indefinitely.

Summer skies have always presented me
with this sense of warmth

As if they're flaming embers of who I am
coming out to dance among the clouds

I suppose that's why I take such comfort
in sitting beneath the stars at night and
watching the sun come to life

In a way it's like watching myself come
back to who I want to be each day

Embracing the good, the bad, the ugly,
and warming it until it melts together in
a creamy balance

I hope that if you're reading this, you
find that balance within yourself today,
and if you need a little help just look
to the sky

I will be there in the clouds reminding
you that you have always known who you
are and where you will go

Life to me often feels like seasons

I know that when winter hits I'll
struggle to keep my composure

Often forgetting I can rely on myself or
those around me when the day feels too
hard

The lack of sun will make the hard
moments tenfold and I'll battle myself
until I finally lay in silence and just
exist for a bit

My mother will worry

Spring will come and I'll begin flutter
back to life, excitedly so

My friends that I've lost contact with
will be surprised at the positive
messages I share with them, simply glad I
made it through another drought

When summer hits, my heart will pound in
my chest so hard the world will think
I'm in love again

It's always my favorite

Fall will come, and I'll board up the windows and prepare once more for my depression to take hold of me as if it has a collar around my throat

I'll enjoy the changes of leaves and the cooler weather, sip on some coffee

And when people ask, I'll smile and say I'm okay

Because I know the season will once again change, and I'll be waiting.

Gentle thoughts rush through my mind
winding their way through my bones, they
litter secrets of certainty throughout me
brushing soft snow around my heart

I crave these moments

Comforting in simple existence

People will light fires in you only to douse them out later

Always bring a blanket to those winter nights and learn to walk away with your value

She reminds me of rose petals

Adorably too beautiful to stare at for long

But comfortable with her thorns

Studious and light she found herself
pushing forward

Seeking for a new road to take each day

When storms washed away the rocks beneath
her feet

She built pathways out of branches with
what she could find

In some ways she always knew she'd find
her way

That little bit of knowledge comforted
her in the moments she felt alone

Always believe in yourself child, you can
climb mountains if you try hard enough

Love changes us

In the most dynamic ways

From teaching us to cater to ourselves

To passing love letters between stealing
glances

We risk it all to be careless

To be reckless

I love that love doesn' t fit in a box

With all of the words in the world we
still struggle to describe it

I wish to always lose myself to battles
of love

Only to discover myself in oceans of it

To hold and cling, to let go

To fear, to embrace

May love never stop finding me

Whenever I swim in oceans part of me
feels like it's coming home

As if the waves have been waiting to open
the door for me

Welcoming me and embracing me with love

Perhaps that's why I cry when I'm
beneath the water

Everything I've ever felt comes rushing
in and the only ones to see me are the
fish in the sea

I write poetry for many reasons

Most would say it' s to express myself

Some would say it' s to confess

But I think the reason I write the most
is to try and understand love and the
things in life I' ve had to witness

Like undressing in front of strangers, I
get shy when one reads my words

But when I' m alone in the mirror, I love
the words and their tiny curves

Money is a lot like love

It comes and it goes

People only adore you for it if it
benefits them

No matter how much you spend there' s
always more around the corner

Please don' t forget to love yourself
when your bucket feels empty and the well
seems dry

Dip it back in and give it another try

You are not alone

I confess I'm not really good at relationships

I often give too much

But I was raised to always give my all in a home that never gave enough

So if you find yourself on the receiving end, please understand I am trying

I struggle to showcase how I really feel and sometime that comes in the form of buying

I don't ever want to buy somebody's love, but I never want someone I love to go without

Sometimes I fear I'm giving too much but I guess one day I'll find out

I wish I wish upon a star

To fall in love with all my heart

To love myself through night and day

To trust my gut through the worst of pain

I wish I wish to find romance

To be unafraid to hold my own hand

I wish for kindness, for truth and light

I wish for a peaceful mind at night

As much as I despise looking back at my
past

I know it's brought me to where I am

It's given me wounds that've healed
into scars so that I can create
storybooks of who I am

Each little dot is a secret I felt

A thought, an emotion, a drop

Bottling them up never felt right from
the start

But writing them down feels like a lot

As draining as it is, it's a way for me
to process

The lessons and losses in life

I only hope to share them to understand
myself better

To keep myself alive

I've never been a fan of rhymes in poems

The way they're meant to have structure

I see them and something inside me just
yells

To break the routine from down under

Break the walls, shut down the organized
thoughts

My mind is not this pristine

I just want to say what I'm feeling
inside

Without somebody wishing to judge me

So I'll write and I'll spit

I'll throw in my two cents

Anything to get what I'm feeling out

I need to write to express myself before
I turn off the lights

Dear self,

You are worthy. You always have been.
Please never leave your value behind.

Sometimes I miss being in love, having somebody to spoil. I know I enjoy my alone time and love is more than a relationship built, but my god it's frustrating trying to date in a world that's digital. There's this idea that communication only exists until you're bored. You don't let somebody know if you're not interested, you just leave. Do people not realize how unnerving that is? How psychologically draining it is? I have no interest in sharing myself with part time partners. I'd rather stay on my own. But sometimes I miss the cuddling and the spontaneous dates, the opportunity to write love letters to somebody other than myself. In some ways it's a shame, and at the end of the day I'm okay. I think I just need to sleep until tomorrow and start again. I'll fall in love with strangers passing and talk to people that don't deserve my time, but at least we're all growing in some ways. At least we're living until we're dying. Love is kinda funny.

It is okay to lose yourself in hopes of gaining a new perspective,

To never be fully sure of your goals or what you're chasing

In some ways, I think that's part of growing

You have to constantly chase knowledge

Constantly chase yourself

To get the most in this lifetime

I hope to always keep myself within my core fundamentals, but to always be reaching out for something new

A new experience

A new adventure

A new chapter in this lifetime

And to always fill it with love and curiosity, opening my arms to welcome the opportunity for growth

Sometimes the messages I read get too loud in my mind

They remind me that there are people watching, waiting to see what step I take next

Some are counting on me to fail

Others are passing expectations on me as if they're writing my story

It's weird to think that somebody on the outside looking in has any interest in seeing me face my daily struggles

Occasionally it feels like a power struggle for my own life

I share my words so that I can feel and let go

I guess in some ways that comes with responsibilities unknown

If anyone is feeling the things I write about or going through similar situations, I hope you always find your footing and come back home to yourself

Water washed over me as if it were the only thing that could clear the marks from within me

It rained so hard that I'm almost certain it left bruises

I only remember tears washing away with it, and a sense of imbalance feeling daunting

There are nights when I look back to falling apart in the shower and I ache to repeat it

If only to recognize my being and experience finding myself all over again

I came to accept myself from the pain I allowed myself to sleep in

The water washed it all away

I feel that I've lived a life of
borrowing emotions to make them my own,
to seem normal in a sense and feel less
alone, but I'm tired of shutting down
the things that I feel, of hiding them in
a dark corner and pretending they're not
real. I breathe a little easier when I
let the light in, when I express my own
feelings rather than focus on the sin. I
have my own thoughts, I have my own
wishes, my own ideas and dreams. My
preferences are different, and they've
always been bottled up, but I almost want
to pop the lid like a champagne bottle
and let them erupt. To see myself in the
way I've always dreamed, to be kind to
myself and let myself be seen. It's odd
that we hide so much of our being, afraid
and ashamed of what people will be
seeing. I just want to be, to love, to
experience. It sounds less scary on
paper, but I'm trying

Five years ago I felt as if I had to be perfect

The perfect daughter

The perfect new adult

The perfect worker

The perfect artist

That direction of some sensation to be perfect all the time made life feel as if I were constantly working

In some ways I think it made a few cracks along my skin and bones, letting the blood of my eagerness and innocence drip like tap water

It felt draining at all times, just to exist in this world where perfection was necessary rather than a trial

Nowadays I feel less eager to please anyone other than myself

I don' t strive to be perfect or to put on this façade so that I appear perfect

I simply exist and do my best

Oh how refreshing it is to feel as if you don' t have live up to any expectations other than your own

I don' t wish to live in a world driven by perfection

I wish to explore a world that is simply always trying to do better and understanding that we all need a break sometimes

My life goal isn' t to be molded into a plaything for others to stare at and watch

I just want to be me

Do you ever feel as if social media is more draining than working all day

It's as if we opened a door for communication and decided to throw a bomb into it

We use it in such horrible ways, demeaning mostly

We make friends around the world and still find ways to feel indebted to them simply because they're there when our thoughts won't go to sleep

There's so odd way of it being an energy source that gets drained too quickly and we just silently plug it in to keep charged

I am so tired of existing on a platform to please others

I simply want to share myself and that be it

You get what you see

My conversations are always transparent, and I never try to dig too deep, but my

thoughts are always hopeful that the
person on the other end of the screen
takes a break when it gets to be too much

I know I've taken more breaks this year
than I can count

I think my body needed them to recover
from whatever online power source spent
years draining them

Social media has so many opportunities
that I think we mistake it for a free for
all

I just wish people left comments of
kindness for others more than they left
remarks of bitter negativity

They pick apart bodies of people they
don't know

They throw flaming bottles filled with
letters of hate to tell somebody they're
not perfect

We all know that, none of us are fucking
perfect

Why does that matter?

Can't we simply exist and express ourselves?

Is it so hard to unfollow somebody or just like their picture so they feel like they're doing a decent job at existing

I'm so exhausted from the comments on sexuality, body shaming, slut shaming - all of it

Why can't we just communicate and share laughter

Why do we have to create this sense of false perfection

I just want to look at a pretty girl, tell her she's pretty, and go about my day

Nothing serious about it

Nothing weird about it

Just supportive kindness so that she knows she's existing and I admire that

Life is so fucking weird with how negative it can be. Please take breaks

I fell in love with a girl once

Not in her looks or her beauty

I fell in love with her words and her
laugh

The way she misunderstood herself

I watched her go through a million
emotions, from happy to angry to sad

I couldn' t help but falling love with
her when she was a little mad

Figuring shit out day by day

Asking questions along the way

She tried to be positive in the worst of
times

Laughed at my dad jokes and silly rhymes

When she was down, it' s as if a light
went out

The entire city experienced a full blown
blackout

and I've never wanted to replace a bulb
so quick

but I'd give her the light in my soul if
she stole it with a kiss

her gentleness fooled all the
townspeople, they never saw her in her
raw

yet for some odd reason she chose me to
witness it

to see her in her all

I think my heart broke the day she showed
me her scars, both physical and mental

I fell in love with her not for her looks
but for her ability to still be gentle

She didn't let the world turn her cruel

She kept moving with a smile on her face

Nobody would know she was hurting inside

All I wish to do is be her aid

I hope she never forgets that she's loved

Even when we go our separate ways

When things get hard I hope she relies on herself to always come back home safe

The darkness is hard, it's never too bright

But life continues to cycle

I hope wherever she goes in this big chaotic world, she's able to find her value as a reason for survival

I fell in love with a girl once

Not for her looks

I fell in love with a girl that was the epitome of love in the best storybooks

Raw

Not simple

A little disheveled

Rarely bitter

At times I wonder if there's been a delay in my heart

You see, I don't always understand how to address my feelings

Often I write them down rather than sharing them with the people that need to hear them

It's the off kilter dysfunction in my brain that tells me to be careful with my words

To only let them be seen if my heart is going to combust

I fall in love while falling away from myself

And often I try to push my emotions back down the throat they're crawling up from

So perhaps there's a delay in my heart

Some miscommunication that doesn't allow me to love the way that others do

To explain my love the way others do

Regardless, I'm okay with that

Biting my tongue has never been my strong
suit

I admit I can often be a little too
honest

I don't hide from the fact that I find
attraction in pretty women, and when they
smile my brain releases too much haze for
me to be anything other than high

I've found that my honesty plays a
strong part in how people perceive me

Either I'm too much or too little

Yet people always seem to think they know
me

It's odd how everyone around me draws
this cartoon image of who I am without
realizing I'm only feeding them the info
I don't mind sharing

They receive a page from a chapter,
nothing more

Nothing less

Never finding out the full storyline

When I first wake in the morning, I'm
always more content with myself. Somehow
I feel that my first breath of the day is
like sitting in shallow water, letting
the miniature waves wash over me in a
sense of something new. I am comfortable,
prepared, able. For a few moments the
voices in my mind aren't restless,
they're appreciative and subtle, almost
thanking me for the rest my body has had.
Rather than pins and needles, my body
feels at peace, and my mind is slowly
whispering that it loves me. These are my
favorite moments. The tiny seconds in my
raw where I simply exist.

Spend time with me softly

Living in present moments that create
echoes

Listen to me intently

As if my words are more than thoughts
hollowed

Time is a construct that convinces us
we'll blossom

I hope to grow old together outside of
the limitations the world has created
so that our love is a timeless, ageless
window of seeing each other for all that
we are and all that we can be

Life often feels as if I'm in a room surrounded by windows

Peeing through each one at different opportunities

The hardest part is pulling back the latches and climbing through to the next adventure

I wonder if I'll find you there

Finding moments of peace is almost
surreal to me

I find myself embracing them as if
they' re a family member I haven' t seen
in years

So ready for comfort

Excited to feel at home within my being

It's been so long since I've been in love with anybody that the idea almost seems like a foreign language

Love is a tongue we can study but never fully master

She found solitude in moments of darkness

Using the lows to wrap around her

Making them become her blanket of comfort

Rather than a chain binding her

Isn' t it odd how we spend our days
chasing after a love we can only wish to
find, rather than loving ourselves and
allowing others to find us happily aware
of everything we deserve without forcing
it

We are never guaranteed another moment in this lifetime

So I am choosing to love myself during the light and dark

For all that I am rather a sliver of my being

Most mornings I find myself sipping coffee, relaxing and easing myself into the day

It seems odd to me that it took 25 years to recognize my value and how deserving I am of breaks

Slow starts to the day have become my favorite because they allow me to understand my emotions for the morning

They allow me to process any leftover feelings from the night before, and to accept where I am

If I'm feeling down or angry, upset or happy, I can break those feelings into tiny journal entries until I feel whole again

I never knew that self care was more than getting up and going to school or work

It's taking time to be with yourself when nobody is watching

It's so much more

I have spent almost 365 days writing
notes to myself detailing the things
I' ve done for myself each day

If therapists didn' t exist, this would
be the closest thing to seeing a
psychologist as I' ve gone

How oddly therapeutic

Nights have taken on the role of feeling like bottles of calmness

I drink them down and bathe in them to feel sane when my heart and mind are heavy

Learning to rely and listen to my own feelings is the best thing I ever learned to do

I suppose you could say I've become immune to my own poison

Comfortable in being desolate with myself at times

Understanding that moments like this shall pass

There's something about learning to admire yourself in the silence that feels like you're truly coming home

I no longer ache when I think of the
future I'm going to have

Nothing seems out of reach

I don't know if that's a sign that
I've finally fallen in love with myself
and the life I live

Or if it's just acceptance that I can do
anything I dream of and still be okay

Somehow the lack of pain makes me feel
less insane

It makes it feel as if I've made it

Everything was worth it

Life is as complex and simple as we allow

I think I've learned this year that I
not longer wish to find the complications
of mistrust in my own being

I simply want to exist as I am, love as
hard as I can, and be kind to the people
and the world I exist alongside

That's not too hard, right?

May I always find value in myself

For I have spent too many years in
adolescence misunderstanding I was more
than I ever needed and everything I ever
wished for all along

DEAR FUTURE

LOVE,

YOU ARE EVERYTHING

Dear Future Wife,

I hope on the restless nights you reach out for me and seek comfort between my arms

We can lay in a daze of laziness and simply exist together if it's what's best for you

When you can't sleep, I hope that you wake me and tell me all of the thoughts ringing in your head

Even when they don't make sense and even when I don't understand

I hope we rely on each other for facing the world when it feels hard

I can't wait to hold your hand and race through life together

Chaos and all

I will kiss you whenever I wish to remind you that you're not alone

When you look cute

When I just want to say I love you in the silence

I hope you understand

Dear Future Wife

I'm sipping coffee thinking of the ways
we will grow together one day

Swirling a milky liquid around, looking
forward to the day we meet

I hope you face a peacefulness so soft
today that you reflect on all of the
things that've made you smile

I hope the world is kind to your heart
today and you feel at ease

We may not know we'll wind up together
yet, but I am looking towards the moments
we will share

Dear Future Wife

Please be kind to yourself when the world
feels heavy

Be gentle with your body as you cleanse
it from the dirt and grime

When you are afraid, turn to yourself and
remember you are always there

Always whole

I pray the world showers you with love
and sincerity

But we both know how cruel it can be

I hope you never lose your sense of worth

I can' t wait to leave you love letters
in the morning before heading off to work

I can' t wait to love you

Dear Future Wife,

Travelling will be different with you

I know I'll sneak pictures of you just to capture beauty as it explores the beauty of a place we've never seen

I'll photograph the adventures we take solely to look back at in disbelief one day

To memorialize the fact that I was able to witness the beauty of the world while falling in love across the map with the most beautiful girl

Dear Future Wife,

Can we lay here a little longer this morning? I just want to spend an extra minute appreciating you, relaxing beneath the sheets with you in my arms next to me. It's the highlight of waking up each day, being beside you. It brings me more joy than I could ever explain. These are the moments I've spent my entire life writing about. Can we just stay here one more minute? I want to inhale you like my first breath of the day.

Dear Future Wife,

The sight of wax on you has my mouth
watering as if I haven't put a bottle to
my lips in years

So breathtaking.

Dear Future Wife,

Do you look forward to nights spent in the kitchen laughing at whatever concoction I've decided to attempt preparing?

I dream about the moments I make you try your damndest to keep your composure, but by mistake I do something silly and you can't help but break out in laughter

Those moments with you will be my favorite

Purely unreal to me until I get to relive them with you over and over again

I'm excited to see what our life together looks like.

Dear Future Wife,

I hope that you never feel resentful towards me for pushing you to be your own entity

I pray that you find independence in your goals and dreams, and you allow me to simply admire you as you accomplish great things

I hope you're comfortable with your alone time, because I could spend hours in my own head without talking, but I promise to come back to you when I'm back on the ground

Could we build each other up and grow together without limiting our capabilities?

Will you let me support you and encourage you, being there only as needed but never taking away from the things you've accomplished?

I hope we find a balance between what we become together and what we become on our own

I hope we can act as partners that stand
off to the side and applaud each other,
always proud and unwavering

I know I'll swallow your love whole that
way

Dear Future Wife,

My mom is going to spoil you. The first day I bring you home she'll spend time teasing me and telling you embarrassing stories. When holidays and birthdays come she'll surround you with gifts, just because she can't help it. She'll spoil surprises out of excitement, but she'll love you. You'll eat more homecooked meals than you've ever eaten when it comes to her, and she'll always convince you to take some home. She'll call you randomly to vent about her day and to tell you jokes. When we take our traditional family vacations, she won't let you pay for anything. Neither will Steve. I hope we have the kind of love that they do. I hope it's always calm and comfortable. That we talk things out rather than argue. My family has a tendency to show love by telling jokes or pranking each other, so don't be shy when it comes to getting them back. My mom will always be on your side when I tease you, and she'll make sure you win.

Bringing you home to everyone is going to change my life as much as you are. I can't wait to share that with you.

Dear Future Wife,

I promise to explore you the way caves in the mountains are explored,

Slowly rather than all at once

I'll listen and try to comprehend the things you tell me each day

And when I'm too stubborn to try, I'll write you a letter with everything I have to say

I may not always get everything right, but I promise I'll try

To learn all there is about you

Starting with one step at a time

Dear Future Wife,

Years of hiding myself away have taught me patience

They've given me the solitude I need to refuse to lower my standards

My mother has always taught me that love should be more than kind

It should grow alongside you as you chase your dreams like fireflies

When I marry my future wife, I hope she sees the love my mother has to offer and feels it wash over her the way I have all of my life

Dear Future Wife,

Can we carve pumpkins on the first of October?

I'd like to make one that's spooky and another that just says I love you.

I will love you in all of your seasons.

Dear Future Wife,

I hope we never feel as if we have to
define ourselves

Living in a box setting with labels and
directions feels so suffocating to me

With whatever we become

I just hope that we chase our happiness
and figure it out as we go.

Dear Future Wife,

As I sit here watching the sun lower itself seemingly beneath the ground

I'm thinking of you

How it'll feel to reach out and run my fingers through your hair

Where we'll we go and what we'll see

I'm thinking of what you'll say when you see me lost in a book or frustrated over words that I can't seem to get right

Will you kiss me when I'm like that?

Just to help me come back down to earth

Dear Future Wife,

I think about holding your hand and my
heart instantly warms up

Dear Future Wife,

I imagine wine nights will be filled with laughter and dumb jokes

I'll learn your favorite drinks just so I can make sure to have them

And I'll make myself like them solely so we can enjoy them together

I won't complain when I get to see you this way

So carelessly abandoned in your walls

At your rawest

I will love you tender on these nights

Between my arms and on my chest

I'll bring you water and make sure you sleep peacefully

Dear Future Wife,

I slept peacefully last night

Relaxing into my sheets with thoughts of us curling up together and reading a book

Maybe eating a granny smith apple as we turn the pages

It felt comforting to rest to the idea of a future with you

Dear Future Wife,

Should we have kids one day, I hope
you'll believe me when I tell you
you're a good mother. I hope through all
of the chaos my voice is what you hear
when you begin to doubt yourself in
parenting and in any aspect of life. You
are more than good enough. You always
have been. Please have faith in yourself
and when you need a break, rest on me.

Dear Future Wife,

Do you prefer beer or wine

Do you like snacks throughout the day or
full meals

Are you a late sleeper or will you get up
to watch the sun come up with me

I can' t wait to learn your interests

The things that make you upset

How you look when you' re stressed and
how you look when you' re tired

Dear Future Wife,

When we start dating you're going to become my taste tester

All of the random recipes I want to try my hand at, you'll be the first person to take a bite

I want you to be honest with me when something tastes like absolute shit

I want us to laugh about my attempt and debate whether or not I should try again

Inevitably I will

Try again that is

I will try until I master each recipe so well that it becomes your favorite dish

Something that we can enjoy together

A way I can do something for you without spending a bunch of money on a gift that's only temporary

At least this will nurture us

Dear Future Wife,

Do you mind if I come home from a long day of working and curl up atop you

There are days when I struggle to exist and doing so is so exhausting that all I wish to do is rest

I'd enjoy resting with you on a day like that

Dear Future Wife,

I promise to bring you breakfast in bed
on the mornings I wake up long before you

I' 11 fix your coffee and prepare your
favorite

Simply as a thank you for existing

For continuing to be around me as I grow
in goals and frustrated spouts

Dear Future Wife,

When we have to face difficult moments together, I promise to hold your hand

I'll run my thumb over the back of your fingers and listen until you've said everything you need

Then I'll take my time to respond without anger or frustration

I'll do my best to calm the harshness in my voice and to prove that I care enough to work with you

Dear Future Wife,

Will you pose for my books so that I can have inspiration when I write

Can you smile at me when I'm so lost in staring I forget you're not a painting on my wall

I want to be so entranced in the simplicity of moments together that I lose track of time and my only thought is how lucky I am to be next to you

Dear Future Wife,

When you meet my puppy, I hope you love her as much as I do

I hope we raise dogs together long before the idea of adopting children comes into play

Just so we can fall in step with each other

With our routines and the simplicity of being domestic

Dear Future Wife,

Share your music with me

I may crack jokes, but I will note every song that makes you smile so that I can make sure to play them when life gets a little hard

Dear Future Wife,

I will collect your heart the way I
collect words

I'll cater to it and build walls around
it with the books I write about it

I won't take the key to your heart,
that's yours to keep

But I will mow the grass and maintain the
land that it lives on

I will take care of you

Dear Future Wife,

As I get ready for bed tonight I'm picturing the day I wake up and we brush our teeth together

Smiling and making goofy faces through the mirror

Oh what a process it'll be, rushing around in the mornings

Falling asleep together at night

There will be so much innocence in a lot of the things I do, just as much as there will be moments I can't seem to control my desires,

But I will always ask for consent and I will always nurture you in every way I know how

Thinking of our future together always fells bright

Like a bulb in my chest that's growing hot from being left on too long

I'm excited for our bulbs to burn together

Dear Future Wife,

Do you question the idea of being with
somebody for the rest of your life?

I do.

It's frightening to think I could rely
on somebody for so long

And I understand if one day you grow
tired of me and my bullshit

I'll be thankful for the time we had
together

But I won't lie and say I didn't hope
we spent forever together

Dear Future Wife,

I wish for you on lonely nights

Dear Future Wife,

I imagine us sitting on a beach laughing with my family, drinks in hand as we rush down to the water to cool off

My family will adore you for making me happy

They'll tease me in front of you to embarrass me and tell you my dirty secrets that I've already told you

I'll pretend to be upset and embarrass them back

We'll go on golf cart rides and spend too much time being lazy

We'll go eat together and talk about how we're eating too much

We'll nap and watch a good show throughout the week, spending time by the pool

My mom will convince you to play this game where she guesses songs from when she was a young adult,

and she'll kick your ass at it

but it'll be so funny seeing her get
excited

You'll fit right in with our sarcastic
replies all week

And I'll look forward to the next family
vacation

Dear Future Wife,

I woke up this morning thinking of how
one day I'll wake up craving you the way
I crave my morning coffee I'll wake up
craving you the way I crave my morning
coffee

You will settle into my soul

Dear Future Wife,

Do you believe romance is dead

I feel like it's changed

It's grown to be something that can be anything we decide it to

Sweet

Sincere

Simple

Extraordinary

Romance is almost like a far off dream that we can cling to whenever we kiss

Dear Future Wife,

I hope we take turns being the leader

Figuring stuff out together and winging
it

Life isn' t meant to be a gift tied
perfectly with a pretty ribbon

I want to rip open that gift and run with
it while holding your hand

One day at a time

Dear Future Wife,

I hope you're as excited as I am

For nights that I will fall asleep to you

For mornings I will wake up to you

All of these tiny moments when we will be at our weakest

Trusting each other enough to rest next to each other

Starting and ending

Beginning and finishing

All of these days ahead of us

Together

Dear Future Wife,

I can't wait to kiss you on the nose

And on the forehead

Innocent yet meaningful

Early in the morning

Late at night

Whenever we're celebrating

Whenever I want

I am excited for the small moments

Where our need for affection is almost too much

Dear Future Wife,

I will build a bookshelf to home the
poetry I write about you

I' ll plan new journals in it so you can
read them at your choosing

Whenever you need a reminder of your
value

Of the things about you I love and the
things about you that I hope you love

You can flip through the pages at your
own desire and always find something that
offers you a soft moment of pure emotion
I had and will have for you

The pages will all be dedicated to you

Dear Future Wife,

I've never been one for jealousy

It's simply something I have no patience for

So I hope that you'll understand if I don't pay attention to small things sometimes

I'll do my best

But the second you or anyone in my life tries to make me jealous I'll choose to ignore it for the sanity of my mind and the comfort of my heart

I won't act out or start an argument over it

I'll simply move forward because it's all I've ever known

I hope you always move forward with me

DEAR FUTURE WIFE,

MY BOOKSHELF WILL SEEM NEVERENDING, AND AT TIMES THAT MIGHT ANNOY YOU

HOW IT'S OFTEN ORGANIZED ONLY BRIEFLY AND THEN RE-ORGANIZED IN A COMPLETELY DIFFERENT MANNER

YOU SEE, I GO THROUGH BOOKS ALL AT ONCE OR NOT AT ALL

I WILL BRING THEM ON TRIPS AND COCOON MYSELF BETWEEN THE PAGES ONLY TO REALIZE LATER THAT I'VE LOST TRACK OF TIME

I HOPE THAT YOU NEVER FEEL NEGLECTED DURING THOSE MOMENTS WHERE I NEED A BRIEF ESCAPE

SOME TIME IN MY HEAD AWAY FROM MY DAILY THOUGHTS

I'LL ORDER HUNDREDS OF BOOKS AT A TIME, SELLING OFF THE ONES I REFUSE TO READ AGAIN SIMPLY BECAUSE THEY DON'T LEAVE A FIRE BURNING IN ME TO GO BACK AND EXPLORE FOR MORE

YOU MAY GET TIRED OF SEEING ME BUY SHELF
FULLS AND LEAVING THEM FOR MONTHS ON END,

I PROMISE I WILL GET TO THEM IN TIME

BOOKS FOR ME ARE MY ESCAPE WHEN MY WORDS
NO LONGER MAKE SENSE

THEY'RE WHAT I USE TO WRITE WHEN I FEEL
LIKE THE LETTERS IN MY BRAIN ARE
SCRAMBLED EGGS THAT'VE BEEN OVERCOOKED

I PROMISE I WILL ALWAYS COME BACK TO YOU
THOUGH

I WILL SHARE MY THOUGHTS AND NOTES WHEN I
FINISH A GOOD BOOK

THEN, WHEN I'VE PUT DOWN THE BOOKS I
WISH TO READ, I'LL WRITE MY OWN

I'LL COMPOSE MY NEXT LOVE LETTER TO YOU

Dear Future Wife,

When winter comes and time seems to slow

I hope your life still seems to glow

I hope we capture the moments we exist

And paint the walls with everything we
wish

Dear Future Wife,

I've never been for the extravagant things

I'm simple mostly

We don't have to go out and fly around the world

We can be lazy sometimes and just curl up

Hold hands, watch movies, casual stuff

When you're tired I'll roll down the bed sheets

Make you a cup of tea

We can just relax and take time slowly

Dear Future Wife,

You may find it funny how I check the door three times to make sure it's locked

Or the way I'll move around and find little things to take to the trash throughout the day, ripping up paper as an excuse to walk that way again

You'll notice little quirks like the way I'll look at my computer and won't type, lost in whatever thought is on my mind

I'll reorganize my bookshelf multiple times, just to have a break from work or to take a pause on the stressful things in life

At times I'll see distant, but I promise I'm still listening

I just get a little lost sometimes, caught up in my head

But I promise you I will always come home to you and meet you in time for bed

Dear Future Wife,

Do you mind if we don't talk sometimes?

I know that sounds a little odd, but I enjoy basking in the silence of somebody's existence,

Just sitting together and doing our own things

Close enough to touch or hold hands but still doing separate tasks

Sometimes I find moments like that better than sex

I find that being able to exist together can be more intimate

You'll notice I'll pause from working or whatever I'm doing to glance at you, and while I won't say anything I'll be thinking of how lucky I am

Content in our silence together

Happy that we are together

Moments of quiet comfort are my favorite

Dear Future Wife,

I want to learn language after language
so that I can write you a letter each day
telling you I love you with new words

So that our love will never dim, and when
it does, I can work to love you in an
entirely new way,

Always trying, always growing, always
loving you

Dear Future Wife,

I've never had the patience for makeup

And I often go through random phases where I try to pretend like I know what I'm doing

But if you're sad or bored, or you just want somebody you can decorate like a clown,

I'll let you put anything on me if I can just state at your beauty and enjoy your smile while you do something you're passionate about

Supporting you and encouraging the things that make you excited will always be a priority to me

I hope I do things that make you feel nurtured

Dear Future Wife,

Will you disconnect from the world with me for a while

Just to watch the stars and make wishes that we'll pursue come morning?

Dear Future Wife,

If you ever feel lonely or as if you're lacking in some way, I hope you talk to me

I may not have all the answers in this lifetime, and I'm more than likely always going to question my own reality, but I will always listen

I'll be your 24/7 around the clock personal service reminder that your value is immeasurable

That you always have room to grow, as we all do, and so long you try you're doing okay

We were never meant to have everything together, so we'll simply seek out what's worth focusing on together

When you need a break, a moment to rest, lean on me and I'll just be with you in silence

We can just exist

Dear Future Wife,

I look forward to finding love in the moments that surround us. In the breakfasts we share, the car rides we take, the music we listen to and every aspect of the things that exist around us while we exist. It's as if discovering love in the things we're around is a new opportunity to fall in love again, with you and with the time spent with you. I hope to fall in love with the pictures we take, the memes we laugh so hard we cry over, and the bad jokes that I will tell nonstop. If I can capture every ounce of love we share and put it in a bottle, it might be better than catching lightning bugs on a summer night. I'll be catching love that I can share with you, endlessly. Effortlessly. Through the good and bad.

Dear Future Wife

I promise not to compare you to those in my past, only to tell you that I'm glad to be in the moments with you

I promise that I'll show my admiration for the things you do even when you think they're simple

You deserve to always see the value that I see in you, and I aim to make it clear so that on hard days you can look to me as a reminder that you are everything

Dear Future Wife,

Thinking of you I always imagine us sitting together working in our creative elements

I can envision looking over at you and getting carried away with thinking how lucky I am to know your mind, your body, and everything you allow me.

Drinking morning tea I will admire your early hour gleam after a night's rest, and I will tell you each time the words pop in my head that you are so incredibly beautiful

I'm looking towards the easy moments with you where we can simply be together and I can confess my love like it's the first taste I've ever loved.

Dear Future Wife,

I hope you never feel as if you have to choose between spending time with me and your friends,

I will encourage you to go out with them,

Pick you up if you all need a ride home,

And check in to make sure you' re safe.

I want you to always enjoy your time with your friends and to be able to come home and feel comfortable telling me about the adventures you went on.

One day we won' t be here, and I hope to never stand in the way between your friends getting to cherish you the way that I do.

Dear Future Wife,

Early mornings when we don' t have work
and we only have each other, I' ll find
comfort in dazing at you through lazy
eyes as I doze off in quiet slumber

I' ll wake back up only to pull you
closer and to contemplate how lucky I am
before falling back asleep into a morning
of restful moments

Those will be my favorite days, where I
can lounge around simply admiring you.

Dear Future Wife,

There will never be a blanket nor a
hoodie nor a sense of warmth better than
when I am holding you

I will always seek out your body in my
arms, a soft form of touching when we' re
sitting side by side

I will always search for your embrace
even when we' re together

Dear Future Wife,

I'm known to bring up odd topics, random theories, and to start discussions on the most random things

I hope you'll find a sense of comfort in the moments I share that side of myself with you

It's the way my mind works and when I talk about these things, I'm feelings a sensation of being home

I hope our discussions always find us returning to each other

Dear Future Wife,

Thinking about the talents and skills I' ll witness you grow with excites me

I imagine that I' ll never have enough words to tell you how genuinely amazed I am at the things you find enjoyment in

I can' t wait to witness your greatness and to spend each day showering you with support the way you' ve always deserved

Dear Future Wife,

You don't know how much you embody the book of what dreams are made of

Dear Future Wife,

When I tell you I love you, I hope that
you never doubt me. If you do, I hope
that you feel comfortable telling me so
that I can take a step away from
everything else that's so oddly chaotic
in life and simply focus on you. So that
I can gain your trust day after day and
always find a way to make you find love
for yourself from all of the ways I will
love you.

Endlessly.

Selfishly.

Selfessly.

I will love you whole.

Dear Future Wife,

Please never stray from conversations that seem tough. If you're uncertain on how to bring something up, you can just tell me you need to talk and not say anything at all until you're ready. We can sit and simply exist together until you find your words. I will not judge you. I will not try to force you into hurrying up the process of how you think things through. I will be beside you until we can work through it together.

Dear Future Wife,

As we find success in different chapters of our lives

I can't wait to celebrate you before turning to a new page and chasing after the next success

Dear Future Wife,

I want to collect pictures of you the way
I collect journals

I want to fill the shelves of our home
with imprints of who you are and who
you've been

Dear Future Wife,

I imagine you standing in the kitchen somewhere in New York or Tuscany

Eating fresh fruit as we discuss where we want to go next

In my mind you're laughing between bites

I'm starting at you in awe trying to think of words eloquent enough to describe your beauty

Taking pictures with my eyes

I hope you don't mind if I steal a bite to eat

Or a kiss

Dear Future Wife,

I often struggle with putting my thoughts into words

I know

That sounds like bullshit

It tends to take me a while to put the ink trickling from my mind onto paper the way that I wish for it to be seen

So please show me patience on the days I am taking my time trying to tell you how much value I see in you

I only want to show you my perspective so that you feel that somebody is always son your side of life

So that maybe just maybe you'll see the great things about yourself too

Dear Future Wife,

You'll notice that there are days where it's difficult for me to get out of bed, more often than not - I'm working on that, I swear. Please know that I am battling my own mind and when I smile at you and say I'm okay it's only because I've held my depression's hand for so many years alone. I will let you in when I can, but I will also stumble and fall on my way to doing so.

Dear Future Wife,

I hope you'll look at my pup and see a
reflection of the love and attention
I've put into taking care of her

That way you know I will do the same for
you daily

Always listening

Always adoring

Always loving and seeking adventure

Dear Future Wife,

My friends are going to think the world
of you

They'll see you for more than my partner

They'll live to tease you with me, just
like my family will, and they'll
encourage you as much as I do

I hope they'll be as strong of a support
system for you as they've been to me

Dear Future Wife,

There are days when I want so badly to meet you that I can' t stand it

But then I remember you are going to hit me with such a force that I spend the rest of my days falling in love with you

And that makes me feel content with waiting

It helps me take a step back and brace myself for the impact

Excitedly patient

Dear Future Wife,

Christmas is one of my favorite times of each year

Growing up my family owned a Christmas tree farm, and I can't wait to tell you stories of it over hot chocolate

The last few years we celebrate like most families, relaxing and giving gifts

The idea of my family spoiling you with affection and presents warms my heart

They will love you entirely, and I will adore the way you fit in

Dear Future Wife,

When it's cold out, I hope you'll wait
for me to come home and wrap you in my
arms, beneath blankets and surrounded by
pillows

Our pup will curl up with us while we
drink glasses of wine or whiskey and
watch the latest show we've chosen to
binge

We'll end the night with me circling
thoughts about you in my journal until my
pen gives out of ink

The nights will feel so cozy with you,
and for that I am thankful

Dear Future Wife,

Will you prefer breakfast or brunch, and if you're like me and love both, will you be excited to listen to my silly humor as we indulge in our first meal of the day?

Dear Future Wife,

My hands will cling to yours when I need to be reminded how to breathe

I will rely on you in the same way that I hope you'll rely on me, always standing by prepared to listen

If I tremble when I speak, please know that I do trust you but still struggle to trust my own words before letting them flow freely

Life hasn't always been kind, but I will always do my best to show you nothing less than kindness and gratitude

We will be like pilots, always traveling to a new destination together, working through turbulence as needed

Dear Future Wife,

I've learned more and more when it comes
to cooking over the last few years

If I could make it happen, with the
exception of life getting in the way,
I'd love to promise that I'll cook for
you each weekend the way my parent's are
always grilling and cooking my favorites
when they invite me over

It would be exciting to do that for you,
and maybe to invite them over so I could
return their favor and they could see how
absolutely amazing you are more often

Dear Future Wife,

It's funny how people come and go in life, and we mourn the loss of them walking away as if they're physically no longer on this planet

As if they've ceased existing entirely

I think that speaks to how much our souls long to connect with each other

If only our minds would catch up on that

Should anything ever drive us in separate directions

I will always hold you close to my heart and be thankful for our time together

Life is unpredictable, but I will always do my best to show you encouragement and support whether we're together or not

Dear Future Wife,

Do you think about how romance is just
like any other word

It's a pre-defined theory that society
has placed virtual wooden walls around,
waiting for somebody to knock them down

In loving you, I will always aim to knock
down those walls so that we can
experience a romance that nobody
could've imagined

Dear Future Wife,

Each month I'd like to buy a gift card for you

Something to store in a box we look at on days we both have free time

For twelve months I want to put random cards in there, and then replace them whenever we use one

Each month I'll ask you to pull a card from the box without looking

Whatever you pull, that'll be our surprise date night

I simply want this to be a way we can be spontaneously planned

A new way for me to spoil you as you deserve

Dear Future Wife,

Should we ever travel separately, I will write you notes over my morning coffee and mail them out before I go about each day

I want to detail the things in each city that remind me of you before I embrace the bustling race to see everything possible

Then, when able, I'll bring you back to those cities with me so I can capture you in picture perfect images simply existing in the most beautiful locations all over the world

Dear Future Wife,

Please be patient.
Please show me grace.

Dear Future Wife,

It's not unusual for me to second guess myself

More often than not I question the decisions I've made and spend time thinking things over for far too long

I promise I will not second guess the way I feel about you

I will always be prepared to tell you how much you mean to me

Even if I have to shout it from the sidewalks

Whisper it across the pages I write

And leave it behind in the sand or snow

You will never be something I second guess

Dear Future Wife,

When we're tired, do you mind if we curl into each other and rest

We don't have to talk or share whimsical thoughts about the things going on

We can simply exist together if you're okay with it

I will adore being together with you in the moments that are quiet just as much as I will love being with you in the moments that are loud

Dear Future Wife,

If I bring up conversations from our past, it's not because I'm upset or questioning what you meant

I will always ask you in the moment when I'm uncertain or don't understand

When I bring up the talks we've had it's because I often replay the conversations I've had with you in my head

They're important to me and I want to soak in every word you say so that I can hold onto you a little bit more

Dear Future Wife,

People say that actions speak louder than words, so I will give you both

I'll give you my words when I want you to hear the way I feel about you or want to tell you for the thousandth time how much value I see in you

I'll give you my actions behind those words so that you never grow doubtful in the fact that you are a priority

I will give you everything I can to nourish and nurture our relationship so that it will always be growing

So that it will always be filled with love and appreciation

Dear Future Wife,

I have dreamed of a life with you for so long

I know that when I realize I want to marry you it' ll be so surreal I won' t be able to hold it in

I will write you a book with my proposal

For your eyes only

Thanking you for loving me the way that you do and promising to love you even more in the days to come

Dear Future Wife,

We are entities circling around the same world, the same universe

Existing to be the best version of ourselves that we can be

I wonder if falling in love with you will feel the way bestselling books feel when they hit number one on the charts

I know it'll feel like the greatest book that's ever written has unfolded right before my eyes

I will never look away

Dear Future Wife,

I wanna kiss you as the sun rises

As if it's my first breath of the day

I want you to know you are my first
thought when I wake next to you and I
will think about your lips until night
comes and I can kiss you all over again

Always starting

Always ending

Always with you

Dear Future Wife,

Poets write books about the things that make them ache

Novelists write books about what they dream of

So what can I write to tell the heavens that I love so you deeply I can feel it in my bones

What am I to call myself other than your lover

Simply writing lines to tell the world that we've fallen in love

Dear Future Wife,

When life gets chaotic let's build a
fire and burn the things that bring us
pain

We can spread a tarp across the floor and
tape it to the floor while we smash old
unusable plates to relive our stress

Whatever chaos we face, we can get
through it together

We will find a way to let go of it and
cycle back to the things that make us
laugh

Dear Future Wife,

I love you.

Simple as that.

Dear Future Wife,

Quarrels are inevitable

Disagreements are inescapable

I promise to always listen and try to
resolve the things that hinder us from
focusing on our own dreams and goals

Life is too short to do anything other
than love you and grow

Dear Future Wife,

You are beautiful

My eyes will tell you that time and time
again

Just as my words will

I hope you always feel stunning in my
presence

Dear Future Wife,

Our texts will mean more to me than you know

I' ll keep them to read on nights we may be apart

Only to turn around and tell you that you are everything

Dear Future Wife,

If the sun never rose again

I hope you know I would still find light
in any room you were in

I would find sunshine in the opportunity
to love you

Dear Future Wife,

Thank you for being you

Thank you for allowing me to love you

Life wouldn' t be enjoyable without
knowing we could do anything in the world
and I would still get to come home to you

Dear Future Wife,

Wherever you are right now, I hope you are finding a thousand new reasons to love yourself

I hope you're figuring out the things in life that bring you peace, happiness, and make you want to run after life ever more.

You deserve the goodness in this world.

Life is filled with moments of confusion, joy, and exploration. To those of you that read my words, I hope you never stop questioning how amazing you are. I hope you find peace in being everything you' ve ever wished for. You are enough. You have always been enough. Please be kind to yourself and pursue the places, people, and things that make your heart beat harder. You deserve everything.

Asa Ray Henson